Mastering Financial Independence

7 Financial Literacy Principles to Establish Your Financial Future

Darian Hall

TABLE OF CONTENTS

Chapter 1: Mastering the Budget

The first was a businessman with an income well over six figures a year. He spent frivolously, never caring to look at how much or how little entered his bank account.

The second was an engineer for a software company, and he hadn't quite made it to six figures yet. He stuck to a strict budget that allowed him so much in different categories of life. He checked his accounts daily and planned how much he would spend weekly depending on the amount he had.

The first man, distraught and sweating, counted over and over on his fingers the remaining balance for the month. *How could it have gone from $15,000 this month to a meger $2,000?* he thought. *Where did all of it go?*

The man wiped his palms and pulled out his phone and notes. All of his bills had gone through, but there were extra, rather large payments that took him a moment to remember. There was a payment for a roundtrip ticket across the country to see a concert. Another large bill was pending for hotel expenses. Countless nights out for dinner went from $40 here and there to a whopping $400 a week.

How did this even happen? he thought again. *I thought I was being careful! How did this all add up so quickly?*

The second man, smiling to himself, placed two fingers down, leaving a remaining three. *Thanks to all the budgeting I've done,* he thought, *I've managed to save an extra $300 for the month!*

The engineer pulled out his phone and notes and began looking at his finances. All of his bills were paid for, and there were a few extra charges that he could easily place in his memory. There was a charge of about $50 for the groceries he bought to make dinner for himself. There was another charge for the new shirt he bought for work. Similar charges, small and placeable, were listed in categories: work, food, groceries, extra, and so on.

With the budget I set, he thought to himself, *I've managed to save what I've earned and still have some left over.*

Years down the road, the same businessman was drowning in his own debt. Credit cards and unpaid loans littered his table in black and white and red ink. All of the money he spent carelessly was suddenly gone. He hadn't set aside any for emergencies, there was no set amount for groceries, and he didn't even have enough to pay for a new shirt for work.

The engineer, however, saved up plenty over time just by not spending all that he had. His budgeting skills and willpower to stick to that budget had earned him enough to let him start planning his future, investing in others', and working his way toward financial independence.

Setting your financial goals at the onset of your journey, the life-long learning pursuit to mastering financial independence, is a pivotal part of the journey. To begin, let's start by defining what is **financial independence**. To some, it means having enough invested savings to cover your annual expenses. To others, it means being debt-free or even being able to retire early. But, in general, it means having enough savings, liquid cash, and investments to live the life you want to live like you want to live it, both now and in the future. However you define it, the goal is to take steps towards reaching it with intentional financial decisions.

Savings Goals and Milestones

So you have defined what financial freedom means to you, now let's define some financial goals so that we have a blueprint on reaching financial independence. Financial goals are cash, investment, savings, retirement goals that we wish to achieve over some specific period. Achieving these goals can be accomplished by coming up with a plan and prioritizing these goals. Some goals may be more far-reaching and require more planning to complete, while others may be more narrow and take less time to achieve. We can sort these goals into 3-time categories:

- **Short-term financial goals** generally last less than a year. These can include; taking a vacation, starting an emergency fund, saving for some home improvement project, and more.
- **Mid-term financial goals** generally aren't achieved quickly but should take only a couple of years to accomplish. These can include; purchasing a vehicle, paying off debts, paying for a wedding, and more.
- **Long-term financial goals** generally require a minimum of a few years to extended periods to accomplish. These can include; buying a home, saving for a child's college education, saving for retirement or early retirement, and more.

To accomplish any of these goals, you can look to establish a **SMART** strategy. **S**pecific, **M**easurable, **A**chievable, **R**elevant, and **T**imely. Be *specific* in defining the goal you wish to achieve. Make sure you are *measured* with your ability to reach the goal, make sure you have the funds, and give yourself enough time to be *achievable*. Make sure the goal is *relevant* in how accomplishing it will make your life better. Lastly, be astute with the *time* you think you will need to reach the goal you set. Approaching your financial goals in this manner won't guarantee you will reach your goals but goes a long way to establishing a solid foundation and game plan.

Managing your finances from the time you enter adulthood will be a continuous learning experience throughout your life. Making sure you reach various goals within the desired time frame requires you to track your pace and know the distance along the way to your destination. However, there are some time-based goals you can strive to achieve to set yourself up financially.

Goals by Age 25

Now is the time to establish healthy financial habits. Leverage the fact that you have time on your side.

- Fully fund an emergency fund
  - Having money set aside for emergencies is generally a good idea.
- Establish your health insurance
  - The current age to be off your parents' insurance is 26; plan ahead to avoid lapses in coverage.
- Being contributing to a retirement account
  - Attempt to contribute what you can now while young to get compounding started for you.

Goals by Age 30

Now is the time to solidify your financial foundation.

- Eliminate student loan debt
  - Attempting to pay off student loan debt as quickly as possible frees up money for other more important uses.
- Save for a down payment on a home
  - If owning a home is a goal for you, look to save 20% for a down payment. Having that 20% allows you to avoid private mortgage insurance (PMI).
- Secure life insurance and establish a will
  - If you've started a family or have any dependents establishing life insurance and wills are worth looking into.
- Contribute 15% of your income to your retirement account
  - Look to increase your contributions to 15%, or no less than 10% if feasible.

Goals by Age 40

You should be established in life at this moment. Now is the time to tackle critical milestones.

- Eliminate all non-mortgage consumer debt

    - Strive to knock out credit card, car loan, and other consumer debt, ideally with student loans.
- Plan for kids college funds
    - Have a plan in place to pay for your kids' college education.
- Having twice your income saved in retirement accounts
    - This will help you keep on track to having enough saved once you reach retirement age.

Goals by Age 50

Continue to establish the foundation you created and build on previous milestones.

- Max out retirement options
    - Talk with a professional for any adjustments that need to happen to stay on track to meet retirement goals.
- Pay extra on your home
    - With all your consumer debt behind you, now is the time to focus on paying off the mortgage.
- Look into long-term care insurance
    - Start getting this security set up for yourself before it's needed.

Goals by Age 60

Here is the home stretch of your financial marathon.

- Fine-tune your retirement goals
    - Finalize retirement goals and when you want to meet them.
- Review your life insurance and will
    - Review your situation to make sure everything is meeting your needs.

4. **Budgeting helps you avoid or get out of debt**

    a. If wealth had a nemesis, it would be debt. Paying someone back (with or without interest) for things you bought that you couldn't afford hampers your ability to develop any wealth. Budgeting helps you plan for large purchases to avoid debt in the first place.

5. **Budgeting enables you to prepare for emergencies**

    a. Life happens, and it's always best to be prepared when it does. Saving for emergency expenses in your budget allows you to avoid financial difficulties. It's recommended to have 3 to 6 months of expenses saved for emergency expenses, and doing that will take intentional saving and budgeting.

6. **Budgeting helps you to save money**

    a. Living on a budget allows you to eliminate wasteful spending, conversely enabling you to save more. In addition, it will hold you more accountable for how you are spending your money, which, if you are trying to develop good financial habits, is critical.

7. **Budgeting allows you to get and stay ahead**

    a. Living check to check, in debt, and having little to no emergency fund is very stressful. However, when you have some financial cushion, are debt-free, and have enough saved for emergencies, you tend to be less stressed and happier with your financial and life outlook. If you want to reach this point financially, you will require a budget to live.

Budgeting rules can be very effective plans of action when you need a blueprint or inspiration to create your budget. Here are two methods that you can use as inspiration for your budget or implement aspects that you think would be effective for your situation.

The 70% rule

The 70% budget rule is a financial principle that will help you spend, save, and invest no matter your income level.

I. *70% is for monthly expenses*

   A. The first thing you need to do is determine your monthly income. This would be everything going into your checking account after taxes, withholdings, or any other money taken out of your paycheck.

   B. Next, determine how much you have for all your expenses. For conciseness, expenses include *EVERYTHING* you spend money on monthly.

      1. Let's assume your monthly take-home pay is $3,000.

      2. 70% of $3,000 equals **$2,100**, ($3,000 x 0.70 = $2,100).

      3. All your expenses should be less than $2,100 a month to be under the 70% goal.

      4. The key is 70% or less. If you can live on less than 70%, then you should do so. The less you spend monthly, the more you can save or invest.

   C. Lastly, categorize all your spending. Notably, creating a spreadsheet is the easiest way to do this. Even if you use cash to pay for everything, the goal is to track every penny spent to see where the money is spent.

   1. There are apps available today, Mint or Personal Captial, to name a few, that can do this for you relatively easily.

D. If you find yourself over that 70% limit, you may need to cut back on some expenses. Start with cutting out unnecessary 'want' purchases until you're within the 70% limit. If these changes still aren't enough, then maybe more significant changes need to be made. For example, sell a car, find cheaper housing, make more money at work or get a second job. The goal should be to do what you need to do to get under that 70% limit no matter what.

E. Dealing with debt should involve pressing debt, pressing debt being revolving loans, and credit card debt. In addition, anything that hurts your credit or costs too much interest a month should be tackled.

II. *20% goes into savings, paying pressing debt should have priority over savings*

A. Staying with the $3,000 example from earlier, 20% of this would be $600 a month. Again, if you can add more here, do so, especially if you have debt you are trying to pay.

B. If 20% is too steep for your current financial situation, start with what you can, and as time goes on and your financial situation changes, adjust accordingly.

III. *10% goes into donations, tithing, investments, retirement, etc.*

A. Staying with the $3,000 example from earlier, 10% of this would be $300 a month. Again, as with the earlier steps, if you can add more here, do so. That 10% can represent any scenario that requires you to save to achieve your goals.

The 50/30/20 Rule

The 50/30/20 budget rule is a financial principle that is an intuitive and simple plan to help people reach their financial goals.

I. *50% is set aside for 'needs'*

   A. Expenses you can't live without are defined as 'needs.' Those 'needs' can include rent/mortgage, car payments, minimum debt payments, insurance, utilities, and more. Half your after-tax income should be used for all your obligations. If you find yourself over that 50% limit, cutting down on your 'needs' or downsizing your lifestyle may be appropriate.

      1. Let's assume your monthly take-home pay is $3,000.

      2. 50% of $3,000 equals **$1,500**, ($3,000 x 0.50 = $1,500).

      3. All your 'needs' should be less than $1,500 a month to be under the 50% goal.

      4. If you can live on less than 50%, then you should do so. The less you spend monthly, the more you can save or invest.

II. *30% is set aside for 'wants'*

   A. Expenses you can live without that are not essential are defined as 'wants.' These 'wants' can include going out to eat, vacations, sporting events, monthly subscriptions, or even decisions to upgrade a purchase such as a new versus a

Free up money from another category to cover it and keep moving.

Why it works

You don't have to be perfect! All you have to do now is commit to the process of planning your spending (Rules 1 and 2) and then sticking to your plan. Then adjusting the plan as necessary, rinse and repeat as needed.

Rule 4: Age Your Money

Step 1: *Spend your money purposefully.*

Step 2: *Consistently spend less than what you bring in.*

Step 3: *Watch the age of your money grow as you continue doing the above steps.*

How it works

You will have nothing to stress about financially if you are spending money you earned last month. Instead, following the other three rules, you'll be more purposeful about your spending, consistently spend less than you make, and be more prepared for the future. Eventually, you'll be able to cover the current months' rent with dollars from the previous month.

Why it works

You aren't stressed because you aren't living paycheck to paycheck. There's no need to waste time and effort matching bills to a specific paycheck. Instead, you pay a bill when it arrives. What's the result? There's plenty of room to breathe. Less focus on today and more on tomorrow.

Establishing a frugal lifestyle by developing a mindset of living off less is not that complicated. The sum of everything you've read so far is how to live below your means successfully. Living below your means can include the following benefits:

- Saving money for the future
- Less stress when a financial emergency emerges
- Stop living paycheck to paycheck
- Overall less financial stress

Making minor changes by distinguishing between what you need and what you want is a financially beneficial habit to put into practice. This habit, if nurtured, can produce positive financial benefits for a lifetime.

Chapter Summary

In this chapter, we discussed what a budget is and how and why you should budget. A solid budget sets the groundwork for productive financial outcomes for any age and any financial situation. Therefore, establishing that framework as soon as possible and utilizing principles that cement it as a lifestyle sets you up to succeed and your finances to be mastered sooner than later.

Chapter 2: Mastering the Emergency Fund

Tightrope walkers stare danger in the eye and walk the thinnest line mankind can traverse. They defy gravity and wow audiences with their magic. But even those daredevil walkers need a safety net, something to catch them if they should fall.

It was this concept that got Mary thinking. She had plenty she could save up for: shoes, a new TV, an upgraded phone, and the list went on. Instead, she remembered the tightrope walker and their safety net.

Every month, she counted her bills and came up with a total, and every month, the total was close to $2,500. She would add that total to a balance of $5,000. This balance was the amount she decided would be the bare minimum she would allow to be in her account. With these two totals added together, Mary had a safety net of $7,500 to work with. When she rose above that safety net, only then she would consider some new shoes or a brand new phone.

Her plan worked perfectly. Month after month, her safety net remained that safe $7,500, and month after month, she saved up more and more for things she wanted.

That was until the car accident.

Thank goodness she had good car insurance, but she had opted for a high deductible with her health insurance. Not only did she have to pay for her car insurance, she had to pay $3,000 to pay off her deductible for the doctor visits and check-ups.

The chunk those expenses took out of her account was a little under $4,500. It just so happened to be under the safety net amount she had been saving up for so long. Not only did Mary get to pay her monthly bills—water, gas, electric, the mortgage, etc.—she also had enough to pay off her medical bills and the expenses toward her car.

It was thanks to Mary's emergency funds that she found herself in the best-case scenario of the situation. Had she spent her money as soon as she got it and never set aside an emergency fund in the first place, the expenses for her medical bills and car would have been too much to handle.

Just like with a tightrope walker, we never know when the rope is going to shake or when our balance will suddenly take a turn to the left or right. When we do fall, the safety net is there to catch us.

Are you prepared for unexpected expenses that may arise in your life? This can be a sobering question that most may not be able to answer with a positive response. An emergency fund is your safety net when a financial crisis arises, and be sure that one will. With an emergency fund, you can survive the situation without putting yourself in a financial hole that may take years to repair.

Paying Yourself First

A fundamental of personal finance is paying yourself first. The idea behind paying yourself first is basic and straightforward. You are storing away some cash by paying yourself first, whether in a savings account or brokerage account (investment or retirement). You want to do this before any expenses, 'needs' or 'wants,' are paid. Thinking of paying yourself as your first 'bill' can help you build wealth over time. Even a modest amount, $50 or $100 per payday, can help you get ahead of the game and on the road to building wealth.

The easiest way to pay yourself first is to automate the process. For example, for an emergency fund having the money automatically go into an account helps avoid the temptation not to fund the account. If automation isn't available to you or you are not comfortable doing so, then disciplining yourself to make regular, steady contributions should be considered. Contributing to an account consistently helps develop a routine that makes you more likely to continue once you see that it works for you.

The psychological aspect of paying yourself first is just as important as the action itself.

Prioritizing paying yourself first tells you that your future is more important than some utility or credit card company. Money can't buy happiness but can provide peace of mind.

Building An Emergency Fund

Unexpected expenses will occur regardless of how careful you are with your finances. The purpose of an emergency fund is to pay for things generally not included in your budget: for example, unexpected car repairs, emergency dental visits, unexpected travel expenses, etc. It can also help pay expenses if your income is disrupted: for example, an extended illness preventing you from working or losing your job. An emergency fund provides financial resilience, allowing you to deal with unexpected expenses without risking your financial security or increasing your debt, i.e., peace of mind.

Apart from financial security, having an emergency fund has other advantages. Here are three benefits of having an emergency fund:

1. <u>It helps keep your stress level down</u>

   Having an emergency fund self assures you to deal with any of life's unforeseen events without adding financial worries to your list.

2. <u>It keeps you from spending on a whim</u>

   The most dependable way to store your emergency money is out of sight. You won't be able to spend the money on a whim if you keep it out of your immediate grasp.

3. It keeps you from making bad financial decisions

   There may be alternative options for getting cash quickly, such as borrowing, but at what cost? Some of the disadvantages include interest, fees, and penalties.

Starting an emergency fund begins with looking at what you spend in a month. What does that look like? Start by estimating your actual expenses such as:

- Housing
- Food
- Utilities
- Health care (including insurance)
- Transportation
- Debt
- Any personal expenses

While excluding any expenses that are not necessities or can be cut from your budget, such as:

- Entertainment
- Dining out
- Subscriptions
- Vacations/trips

More than half of Americans (or 51 percent) have less than three months' worth of expenses covered in an emergency fund, according to Bankrate's July 2021 Emergency Savings Survey. That total includes 1 in 4 Americans (or 25 percent) who indicate having no emergency fund at all — up from 21 percent in 2020 (Foster, 2021).

The excepted rule of thumb is to have three to six months of living expenses in an emergency fund. However, the proper size of your emergency fund will most likely change over time as your monthly expenses change. Therefore, if feasible, it may be wise to expand your emergency fund, especially for scenarios where having more in your savings could benefit you, including:

- *During a recession*—when unemployment rates are higher, and the length of unemployment is generally longer
- *High-risk employment*—in an industry where layoffs are common
- *Erratic income*—income from unsteady employment

Most people should save at least six months' worth of living costs in today's volatile economic times—preferably more. Having this as a regular expense item in your budget ensures that you are saving for emergencies and not spending that money carelessly. Six months may seem like a tall task, but you will eventually meet this goal with consistent contributions over time.

When to use your emergency fund should be as straightforward as possible. For example, emergencies can be defined as circumstances that occur unexpectedly, such as:

- Job loss
- Essential home repairs
- Medical expenses not covered by insurance
- Major car repairs

These situations should only be unexpected events that require money that you haven't saved to pay off. While unplanned financial opportunities may occur, you should either have more than the minimum in your emergency fund or establish another dedicated account for these situations.

Where to keep your emergency fund should be straightforward as well. The most critical aspect is easy accessibility for the money. A reasonable interest rate would be icing on the cake for the account. Of course, all have their pros and cons on what they offer. Here are some options for where to keep your emergency fund:

CD

Bank certificates of deposit are FDIC-insured up to applicable limits and offer a fixed rate of return.

Pros:

- Offer better interest rates than a standard savings account
- FDIC-insured up to applicable limits and offer a fixed rate of return

Cons:

- Offer less flexibility
- You may have to wait until its maturity date to pull money out
- If you withdraw money early, you may have to pay a penalty

Savings account

Savings account at your bank or credit union.

Pros:

- Has the best account accessibility
- Most accounts offer interest rates

Cons:

- Typically offer the lowest interest rates of any account (generally less than 0.5%)
- Interest rate falls well below the inflation rate, so your money loses value year over year

Treasury bill

A Treasury Bill (T-Bill) is a short-term debt obligation backed by the U.S. Treasury Department with a maturity of one year or less.

Pros:

- The longer the maturity date, the higher the interest rate that the T-Bill will pay to the investor

Cons:

- T-bills have interest rate risk meaning there is a risk that existing bondholders might lose out on higher rates in the future

Investment account

An investment account offered from a brokerage company.

Pros:

- Depending on the types of investment and returns of those investments, it can give better than average returns and beat inflation

Cons:

- Lowest accessibility of other accounts
- Depending on the types of investment and returns of those investments, it can give less than average returns

The best way to pay for emergencies has been what we've been discussing; a dedicated funded account kept in an easily accessible manner. Focus on one of those methods and avoid these five ways to pay for emergencies at all costs:

1. **Credit cards**

   Emergencies are never welcomed, and compounding the situation by paying more than necessary makes it worse. Thinking about the interest you will pay from your card, how it will affect your credit score, potential late fees, or your card limits are not things you want going through your head during an emergency.

2. **Withdrawing from retirement accounts**

   On a $10,000 withdrawal, withdrawing this money could seriously impact your ability to reach your retirement goals. $10,000 may not seem like a lot, but missing out on the years of compounding could result in double-digit losses in your overall account balance.

Using the above example, on a withdrawal from a tax-deferred account, i.e., traditional IRA, 401k, or a 529, you will have to pay a 10% penalty in most cases. In the 22% tax bracket, it will run you about $3,200 of total taxes and penalties, leaving you with around $6,800 left for your emergency.

3. **Depending on family or friends**

   We all have different family and friend situations. So why would you want to possibly, negatively affect a relationship with someone you care about over money? Unless you can guarantee to pay them back in a timely manner, this should be a last resort.

4. **Insurance**

   Insurance usually involves claims, deductibles, being partially covered, etc. These actions are generally timely in moving down the path to receiving the money you need. Insurance should be used for the uses typically required; medical, vehicle, home, life, etc. In other words, insurance is not a great idea to use for an emergency.

5. **Selling risky investments**

   By definition, an emergency is not expected—so paying for an emergency with stocks or bonds sort of defeats the purpose of investing in the first place. Selling assets at a loss affects your bottom line. While selling assets while up has tax implications, also affecting your bottom line. The point, investments are not and should never be the vehicle used for emergencies.

Avoiding Lifestyle Inflation

When people have more money, they are often more likely to spend it. People's spending tends to increase as they advance in their careers and earn higher salaries; this tendency is known as **lifestyle inflation** or **lifestyle creep**.

One reason this happens is the mentality of '**keeping up with the Joneses**.' This concept is the act of feeling compelled to match the spending habits of friends, family, or associates to appear to be doing as well as they are or appear to be. This can become evident in multiple areas of your lifestyle, including vacations, dining out, entertainment, clothing, etc. Despite the appearance, the Joneses may be living check to check and in financial trouble.

Another factor could be a sense of entitlement. For example, you may feel justified splurging on yourself and buying nicer things because of the hard work you've put in to earn your money. While this isn't inherently a bad thing, rewarding yourself too much for your hard work can be detrimental to your current and future financial health.

As your professional and personal situation evolves, some increases in spending are natural. However, without careful spending decision-making, most of us will fall into the trap of lifestyle inflation. The desire for convenience and comfort is normal. But don't allow it to get in the way of your long-term objectives. With this in mind, let's discuss how to avoid lifestyle creep as much as possible.

1. **Be aware of your spending choices**

   Small spending decisions might add up to a fairly expensive lifestyle over time. Consider the reasons why you are adding a new expense to your budget. Is it important? Or is it contributing to lifestyle creep without adding any long-term happiness to your life?

2. **Do the math of any raise**

   When you get a raise, do a deep dive into the money to see how much of a boost in spending you actually are getting. Then decide whether the boost in cash you got is worth an increased lifestyle.

3. **Treat yourself—within reason**

   There's nothing wrong with splurging on yourself now and then. The key is not to go overboard or turn this into a regular expense. Instead, try treating yourself as a reward for some financial goal met or some other achievement.

4. **Budget for indulging spending**

   While I'm not trying to stop you from enjoying life and spending money on yourself, if this is what you choose to do, then do it intelligently. Add a specific amount per month to your budget to account for this excess spending and attempt to balance lifestyle and financial goals.

5. **Gradually add significant changes to your budget**

   When adding new lifestyle expenses, focus on adding one at a time. Adding one at a time allows you to gauge whether the changes are beneficial to you and add any value to your life. If it does, then keep doing it. If not, then let it go.

6. **Find friends with the same goals**

   It's always easier to do what you need to do when you are around like-minded individuals. Finding others that share your financial goals can make the journey easier and not blow your budget for the month trying to 'keep up.'

7. **Automate your savings**

   Automating your savings, emergency fund, or investing just makes life simpler. Knowing that you've already put your money in those accounts before any splurging or excess spending can somewhat ease your mind about that extra spending.

8. **Avoid debt**

   Putting yourself in debt to engage in lifestyle creep is counterproductive and a sign that your spending may be out of control. Trapping yourself in a paycheck to paycheck cycle can be hard to get out of and ideally should be avoided. If anything, any extra debt should be tackled with any excess money.

9. **Setup and use a budget**

   A budget can assist you in keeping track of your spending and staying on target financially. In addition, implementing a budget is the most effective method of avoiding lifestyle inflation.

Chapter Summary

In this chapter, we discussed the importance of paying yourself first and having an emergency fund. Being prepared for those unexpected life situations saves you lost sleep and lowers stress during those moments. We discussed lifestyle inflation and effective ways to manage and avoid it. If utilized in your life, these principles set you up to succeed and your finances to be mastered sooner than later.

Chapter 3: Mastering Your Debt

Reece sat with his other teammates, the menu for *Sage Eiko* flashing on their screens. He stretched and rubbed his hands over his face.

"You alright?" one of them asked.

Reece looked over and nodded, distracted. "Yeah, just thinking," he replied.

"Oh, about heading to Japan?" asked another. She picked up a water bottle and twisted the cap as she spoke. "Still haven't found a place?"

That was the excuse, at least. "Yeah, not yet." He sat up and started up the game with the others.

An old man glided across the playing field, his movements the smooth and graceful workings of a master. He placed his hands together and bowed. "Greetings, student. I hope you have rested well. You have much to learn."

Truth be told, Reece had not slept well at all. He had a lot on his mind. He'd finished his studies but couldn't be placed in the States. He would have to go to Japan and set up there, which involved finding accommodation, planning the transit, and learning about the food and entertainment culture and adjusting his expenses accordingly. This was the dream offered to him right upfront, but he couldn't go because he was still paying off the student loan that had made all this happen.

"What's the play?"

"Monsters."

The numbing act of playing with his team was enough to force the butterflies from his stomach, but the undeniable situation was still there: He was still in massive amounts of debt, and he still wasn't in Japan.

One of his teammates groaned. "Ah, I did it again..." he mumbled. He typed something in and tapped a button with finality.

A pop-up appeared on his screen. "Loan extra mana?"

It felt a little too personal. He'd recently considered taking out a low-rate personal loan to help him pay off his student debt. Some people had vehemently disagreed with his decision, and it had put him on edge.

Then Eiko appeared once more.

"It is important to be aware of your situation and what may be limiting you. Don't be afraid to try something new to handle obstacles differently."

The victory music echoed through the arcade. The four decided to end on a winning streak and began to log off.

Reece took out the personal loan and paid off his student debt. Reaching a milestone pushed him to pursue extra work in his field without being placed, and he managed to pay off the loan quite quickly. Soon after, he applied for a position in Japan and managed to be placed at a company that would cover his accommodation. They also would pay for further studies relating to the work.

And so Reece went to his dream destination to study once again.

Most people will be in debt at some point in their lives. However, not all debts are created equal, and some are viewed as higher quality than others. While debt can take many forms, all personal debt (not corporate or government debt) can be classified into a few categories, including secured debt, unsecured debt, revolving debt, and installment loan debt.

Types Of Debt

Consumer debt refers to personal debts incurred due to the purchase of items for personal use. This debt can include credit card debt, auto loans, mortgages, school loans, and more. These are in contrast to other obligations such as those utilized for business investments or debt incurred from government operations. Consumer debt can be grouped into:

Secured Debt

Secured debt requires some form of collateral. The lender requires a credit check to determine how responsibly debt has been managed, but the asset is committed to the lender if the borrower fails to return the loan. If the loan has defaulted, the lender can seize the asset purchased with the loan.

> **Types of loans:** *auto loans, home loans, secured personal loans*
>
> **Interest rates:** *Lower interest rates generally based on creditworthiness*
>
> **Paying it off:** *Generally, loans can have a set amount, number of payments, and years*
>
> **Tax implications:** *Generally none*
>
> **Credit score ramifications:** *On-time payments help your credit score*

Unsecured Debt

Unsecured debt doesn't require any collateral. When a lender provides a loan with no security, the lender relies only on the borrower's ability and commitment to repay the loan. Generally, unsecured debt carries higher interest rates because the lender has to go to greater lengths to reclaim any money owed from a default.

Advantages/Disadvantages of Consumer Debt

Consumer credit allows people to buy products and services immediately and pay for them later. It provides consumers with spending freedom and, in certain circumstances, benefits and incentives. While consumer debt can have its advantages, there may be some pitfalls if misused as well.

Pros:

- Increases consumer spending and production, growing the economy
- Debt used for education can be considered good debt as it can allow for better-paying jobs for the person in the future
- Allows for financial flexibility; allows someone to pay for something now if needed rather than later once you have the funds

Cons:

- Interest can be high based on the type of debt; the average annual interest rate on credit cards in the United States hit 21% in 2014
- General items purchased do not typically provide utility or appreciate in value, which may justify taking on the debt
- If not appropriately managed, consumer debt can be financially devastating and hurt an individuals credit score, hindering future ability to borrow money
- The temptation to overspend can sometimes cause us to go into debt over wants rather than need purchases

Paying Off Debt

Debt collection organizations often employ debt collectors; however, some work independently. Credit cards, medical bills, car loans, personal loans, business loans, school loans, and even overdue utility and cell phone bills are among the debts collected by debt collection companies. The law limits the methods by which debt collectors can contact debtors and the time and number of times they can do so. The law that sets these limits is the Fair Debt Collection Practices Act (FDCPA).

Fair Debt Collection Practices Act

The Fair Debt Collection Practices Act (FDCPA) is the primary federal law that governs debt collection practices. The FDCPA prohibits debt collection companies from using abusive, unfair, or deceptive practices to collect debts from you. Only third-party debt collectors, such as those who work for a debt collection agency, are subject to the FDCPA.

The FDCPA **covers** the collection of:

- Mortgages
- Credit cards
- Medical payments
- Other debts mainly for personal, family, or household purposes

The FDCPA **does not cover** business debts. It also usually does not cover collection by the original creditor to whom you owe money.

The best way to avoid debt collectors and dealing with any headaches that comes with them is to pay any debts you owe on time. Here are six strategies that are generally used to pay off debt.

Debt Avalanche

Using the debt avalanche strategy, you pay off accounts from the highest interest rate to the lowest.

Step 1: *Make the minimum payments on all accounts*

Step 2: *Put all extra money towards the account with the highest interest rate*

Step 3: *Once the high-interest rate debt is paid, start paying additional money towards the account with the next highest interest*

It might take some time to see progress this way, but once you gain momentum, you will see the account balances going down while your net worth rises.

Pros:

- It will help you pay less in interest on the debt, therefore, paying less overall

Cons:

- It will take longer to see progress on your debt amount going down

Debt Snowball

Using the debt snowball strategy, you pay off accounts from the smallest balance to the largest balance.

Step 1: *Make the minimum payments on all accounts*

Step 2: *Put all extra money towards the account with the smallest balance*

Step 3: *Once the smallest debt is paid, start paying additional money towards the account with the next smallest balance*

This is a popular choice because of the ability to get early victories. In addition, getting accounts paid off is a powerful motivator to keep paying off debt.

Pros:

- You get little wins each time you pay off an account that can motivate you to continue
- Potential to improve your credit score more quickly as you can lower your credit utilization and reduce the number of account balances

Cons:

- You will end up paying more over time because of interest

<u>Balance Transfer</u>

A balance transfer refers to credit card debt and how to transfer debt from one card to another. For example, if you have a high-interest rate account, you can transfer its balance to a card with a lower interest rate.

> ***Step 1:*** *Identify cards where you are paying interest on a balance*
>
> ***Step 2:*** *Decide how much you can or want to transfer*
>
> ***Step 3:*** *Apply for a new transfer balance card, ideally one with 0% APR on balance transfers within a specific time period*
>
> ***Step 4:*** *Transfer any balances from the older card to the newer*
>
> ***Step 5:*** *Pay off the new card balance within the 0% period of the new card*

With the new card will come more credit available at your disposal. So don't use the newly acquired card to rack up any new debts.

Pros:

- This can work well with the debt avalanche method as a strategic method of reducing the interest rate of your highest interest card
- Many cards offer 0% APR introductory periods lasting from 6-18 months, giving you quite some time to pay the balance off before having to pay any interest

Cons:

- The temptation may arise to create more debt on the new card issued

Pros:

- Can sometimes pay 50% or less of the original balance

Cons:

- You may still have to pay taxes on the forgiven amount

Bankruptcy

Bankruptcy can offer a fresh start but should only be used as a last resort as it can devastate your credit.

Step 1: *Examine your debts and determine your ability to pay them off*

Step 2: *If you think it's not feasible to pay all your debts, begin researching bankruptcy attorneys in your area*

Step 3: *Once you find an attorney, you will need to submit comprehensive documentation of debts, credit cards, loans, bank accounts, assets, personal property, and other financial information*

Step 4: *Your attorney collects your information and files the bankruptcy with the proper authorities*

Step 5: *Filing a Chapter 13 bankruptcy requires you to make monthly payments for 3-5 years*

Step 6: *When the bankruptcy is discharged, the creditors will write off the included debts, and you will no longer be responsible for them. Chapter 7 filings can be discharged within 3-4 months, while Chapter 13 filings can take 3-5 years*

Two types of personal bankruptcy

Chapter 7: often requires relinquishing of some property

Chapter 13: allows you to keep your property

Pros:

- Can give you a fresh financial start

Cons:

- It can be a long, expensive process—including attorney and court filing fees
- You will have to attend credit counseling approved by the department of justice
- Filing for bankruptcy can affect you mentally because of the stigma of bankruptcy

Chapter Summary

In this chapter, we discussed the various types of personal debt that you can accrue. Generally, you want to be debt-free, but there are circumstances where having debt can be looked at as a positive. For all those non-positive debt scenarios, we discussed the Fair Debt Collection Practices Act and went over six debt repayment strategies you can implement to take care of any debt.

Chapter 4: Mastering Your Investment Knowledge

There was once a man named John. He started his own company that he raised from the ground up, and he had gotten to the point where he had choices as to what to do next. He ran it by three friends who all advised him differently.

"Sell your company," said the one. He had his own company which was doing exceptionally well, and he had decided to sell and retire early. It was a good decision on his part, and he was able to relax with the money he earned with his family.

However, John wasn't sure if this was the right decision for him, as he was a bit younger than this friend.

"Expand your company," said another who had done exactly that. The friend's second branch was thriving, but he had the resources to expand and make sure that everything was up and running soon after the launch.

It may not be as easy for John, who owned a start-up in comparison.

"Invest your money," came the third reply.

This friend had no company of his own, but he had advised the others on best practices many times before. It was thanks to his advice that their businesses thrived. John hadn't forgotten how much value his words held.

After much thought, John decided to invest. It made more sense because he could always grow the company later, and he would also be more equipped to deal with it.

A few years later, John had the resources necessary to expand the way his friend had suggested. He even had plans to later sell the company and retire like his first friend suggested. His plans seemed airtight, but he wanted to be sure it was the right decision.

John went to an old cafe to meet the friend who had advised him so well. He thanked him and asked him what he had in the works. Apparently, he was pitching to different investors as he had a concept, one that he'd had for some time. After all these years, John didn't expand after all.

He invested in his friend's company.

Historically the most effective method to building generational wealth has been investing in the stock market. So developing your knowledge and experience in investing can pay huge dividends throughout your working career. Paying yourself first, learning how and where to start investing, and staying disciplined will be essential aspects of developing the investment knowledge you are trying to grow.

Paying Yourself First (Investing)

A fundamental of investing is paying yourself first. The idea behind paying yourself first is straightforward and the same principle as saving for an emergency fund. Also, the same as the emergency fund, think of paying yourself as your first 'bill' to building wealth and growing your investment account(s). Starting with small amounts of money can help get you started, but as your financial situation improves, increasing the amount you can contribute will reap the rewards for your accounts as time passes.

How To Start Investing

As long as you can generate income, investing can be beneficial, but ideally, you want to start as early as possible. For example, if you started at 18 and invested $300 every month into an S&P

500 index fund with an average return of 8%, you would see an investment balance of $1,047,302 after 40 years. Conversely, if you start at 28 with the same amount invested monthly into the same fund with the same average return. You would see an investment balance of $894,215 after 30 years. Those extra ten years in the market added $220,000 to your investment balance. Time in the market is your friend when investing.

The best way to start investing while young is to get your finances in order. Try following these steps to get started:

1. Determine how much to invest each month

- **Developing a basic budget.**
    - Before opening any investment account, it's best to determine how much money you can invest each month. Determine your monthly expenses and develop a budget to see how much you can invest each month.
- **Start and grow an emergency fund**
    - The excepted rule of thumb is to have three to six months of living expenses in an emergency fund. Of course, this amount will change over time as your financial situation changes. But it is wise to start one early so that you won't have to take on any debt to cover it when an emergency arises.
- **Pay off high-interest debts**
    - Your focus, in the beginning, should be to pay off high-interest bad debt before going all-in on your investments. The majority of consumer debt is bad debt, and it makes no sense to invest for an 8-10% potential return only to have to pay that required 15% interest rate on some credit cards for purchases that didn't matter.
- **Don't miss the match**
    - The only exception to the rules above is your employer-sponsored retirement accounts. If the company you work for offers an account match, the minimum you should invest, even while

paying debts, is the company match amount. This is free money that is an immediate return on investment. Never miss out on free money!

2. Leave your investments alone

Value investors, or investors that buy and hold investments, should be your thought process as an investor. You should be aiming to keep your assets for 5, 10 years, or longer to benefit from investing. Conversely, **timing the market** involves predicting when the market will go up or down and buying or selling in investments to try and turn a profit. Market timing is viewed as a strategy that doesn't work and won't produce consistent positive returns. Especially if you are a younger investor, let the market work for you by consistently contributing to your accounts every month.

3. Understand investment basics

Stocks

Stock funds typically carry the most significant risk as well as the greatest potential returns. When you buy a stock, you buy a small piece of ownership of the company selling the stock.

Bonds

Bond funds are typically less risky than stock funds. A bond is a loan to a company or government agency usually paid at a fixed interest rate. Because they are less risky, they don't grow in value as much as stocks do.

Real estate

Dealing with real estate can be a high-risk activity but can grow wealth more quickly. For example, you can purchase a property to rehab and then resell or rent out, generating income. Or you can invest in a **real estate investment trust (REIT)** which are closed-end investment companies that own assets related to real estate such as buildings, land, and real estate securities.

Asset allocation

Asset allocation is how you split your investments across asset classes such as stocks, bonds, and other asset classes. Your age, investment goals, and risk tolerance all play a role in determining an appropriate asset allocation. You can use your asset allocation as a guide for your investing strategy once you've found one that fits your investing style.

As with your emergency fund, you want to try to invest as much as you can when first starting, and as your financial situation improves, keep increasing that amount. Again, starting as young as possible is essential as it allows your money the most time in the market and for compounding to work for you. **Compounding** is the process where interest is credited to an existing principal amount and the interest already paid. In effect, it's interest on top of interest, which is to magnify returns to interest over time. Allow compounding to work for you as soon and as long as possible.

Where To Start Investing

While you are still young and can leverage the stock market, you generally want higher returns stocks, index funds, mutual funds, or ETFs(exchange-traded funds) provide. There is inherently more risk with these funds but higher returns as well. Usually, slower-growing investments like bonds and CDs(certificates of deposit) are utilized to maintain investment growth and not to grow it. As a result, over time, those stock-type funds well outperform their less risky counterparts.

Standard Brokerage Account

A stockbroker is an entity that facilitates the buying and selling of marketable securities like stocks and exchange-traded funds (ETFs). You can open a **brokerage account** through a stockbroker, which is a specialized financial account designed to hold investments and cash. These accounts are also known as "taxable accounts."

<u>Mutual Funds</u>

A mutual fund is an investment that gathers money from investors to purchase stocks, bonds, and other assets. A mutual fund aims to create a more diversified portfolio than the average investor could do independently. A professional fund manager purchases a mutual fund's securities. They are a great way to start investing and getting diversification across hundreds of companies, though some may have high minimum investments to buy them.

<u>Index Funds</u>

Index funds are stock baskets that track a segment of the stock market, or the entire market in some situations. These funds are made up of assets that correspond with a major market index such as the Standard & Poor's (S&P 500) or the Dow Jones Industrial Average (DJIA), intending to mirror the risk and returns of that index. Various indexes being real estate, technology, gold, healthcare, and others.

<u>ETF Funds</u>

An exchange-traded fund is a sort of investment fund that is also an exchange-traded product, meaning it can be bought and sold on stock markets. These funds can be traded like stocks but offer the diversification of mutual funds. ETFs can also be built to track specific investment strategies. Compared to mutual funds, ETFs tend to be more liquid and cost-effective. Generally, you can find ETF versions of mutual funds that are more cost-friendly.

Importance Of Discipline

One of the most helpful character attributes our parents taught us growing up should have been being disciplined. This one trait carries into every aspect of our adult lives as either a detriment or benefit. It's a detriment when we don't incorporate it into our lives to make us more productive and level-headed concerning things we do. Conversely, it benefits us positively when we do.

When concerning investing, building the habits necessary to create and sustain those beneficial investing habits can center on three areas:

1. <u>Understanding the necessity to invest</u>
    a. You don't want to wake up one day older, and the only thing you have to your name is a job and a mortgage without any options of pursuing any of your passions or being able to take time off work.
    b. Educating yourself about the consequences of not investing should light a fire under you to do something about now rather than later if you find yourself caring about the consequences.
2. <u>Understanding your current cash flow</u>
    a. Review the information on budgeting from earlier chapters; focus on discovering your monthly spending limits.
    b. Cut out the things that don't add any value to your life if you find yourself overspending.
3. <u>Understanding the importance of automation</u>
    a. Automate your contributions to your various accounts that way; it's out of sight, out of mind.
    b. Over time, increase the amount you contribute as your financial situation improves, ensuring you are putting money away for the increased lifestyle cost.

Chapter Summary

In this chapter, we discussed how paying yourself first should be the first 'bill' you pay to begin growing your investments. Next, we discussed how to start investing by determining how much to invest a month, the importance of leaving your accounts alone, and understanding some investment basics. Then, we discussed where to start your investment journey and some fund types to research. Finally, we discussed the importance of discipline and how developing that muscle could affect your overall investing journey.

How to address:
Watching your health and adopting a healthier lifestyle before any issues arise can help mitigate rising insurance costs.

Higher Medical Expenses

The standard American diet (SAD) can lead to more health problems, including high blood pressure, heart disease, and diabetes. These conditions and others will lead to increased doctors visits and other procedures. At the same time, they require monthly maintenance to live with these issues. How much you pay each month is determined by your insurance.

How to address:
Again, adopting a healthy lifestyle will benefit you now and as you age. But, prevention is the best option compared to maintaining a health issue.

Ability to Work Before Retirement

The longer you can work, the more you can theoretically save for retirement. While people may choose to retire early, many early retirees do so because of health reasons. Less affluent retirees are more likely to cite health reasons for early retirement than higher-income workers. These lower-income retirees have jobs that require significant physical labor, and as they age, they are no longer able to handle the demands of the job.

How to address:
Addressing health concerns can prolong your ability to retire when you are ready.

Ability to Live Independently

We all want to live independently, at home, till the end of our lives, but this is not always possible. While some medical conditions, such as strokes, are simply a part of getting older, poor health and an improper diet can increase the risk of developing a variety of other ailments. Issues such as Alzheimer's, dementia, fractures from falling can require long-term care in your home or you living in a residence where care is available.

How to address:
Preserving your health while young will benefit you as you get older. So take the time to focus on being as healthy as possible to reduce any issues that affect you as you age.

Prioritize Your Health

One of the significant aspects of your life you should prioritize constantly is your health. Everything you work for is meaningless if you don't have good health. It's practically impossible to separate finances and health. After all, health care is costly, and earning money is much easier when you're in good health. You may believe that you simply do not have enough time to focus on healthy habits such as a well-balanced diet, exercise, and sleep. However, if you consider the numerous financial benefits of prioritizing your health, you may reconsider:

<u>Employer Incentives</u>
Employers are increasingly realizing that having healthy personnel is good for business. Whether or not employers care about their employees' health, offering financial incentives for good behaviors is a solid start that more companies should adopt. Those incentives can include:

- Reimbursements for gym memberships and health-related prescriptions
- Onsite fitness centers or various offerings such as yoga or fitness classes
- Free or discounted health coaching
- Bonus for never smoking or quitting smoking
- Insurance premiums for meeting health standards

Why not take advantage of any or all of these incentives if your employer offers them? You might save a lot of money on your insurance or get cash bonuses or gift cards for adopting better behaviors.

Miss Less Time from Work

It's a logical conclusion that healthy people miss less time from work being sick for the most part. Adopting healthy habits may lead you to get sick less frequently. If you have a job that doesn't pay you unless you show up for work, taking sick days can affect you directly. Some employers allow sick days to carry over yearly, allowing you to save those unused days for when you need extended time. Employers value employees who do not miss work frequently due to illness. According to the CDC, the average cost of missed production due to absenteeism is $1,685 per employee.

Healthy Habits that directly Improves Finances

Here are three healthy habits you can incorporate into your life today to improve your health and finances.

1. Prioritize your health by getting enough sleep

   The average adult needs 7 to 8 hours of undisturbed sleep per night. Prioritizing rest[1] can impact you financially as well:

   - Its easier to maintain focus throughout the day, improving productivity
   - Generally improves your mood and disposition
   - Can lower your risk of obesity, Type 2 diabetes, heart disease, and high blood pressure
   - It can affect your immune system allowing your body to fight germs more effectively
   - Generally gives you more energy throughout the day

2. Prioritize your health by exercising regularly

   Exercise brings many of the same advantages as adequate rest. In addition, exercising helps maintain healthy body weight, build muscle tone, improve energy levels, and improve your focus, and more. Exercising puts you less at risk of serious diseases like cancer and heart disease. Getting plenty of physical activity can also reduce feelings of depression; mental health is also an essential part of our overall well-being. All of which can make you eligible for your employers' health incentives.

3. Prioritize your health by having a healthy diet

   Having a healthy diet is one of the best weapons against illness though eating healthy isn't always easy for us, especially in our current society. Much like exercise and sleep, healthy foods provides vitamins, nutrients, and numerous benefits:

   - Lowered risk of Type 2 diabetes, certain cancers, heart disease, and obesity
   - Better dental health
   - Stronger bones and muscles
   - Higher energy levels

   One of the pitfalls of eating healthier has been the cost. However, contrary to popular belief, it's possible to eat healthy on a budget; there are plenty of healthy and cost-effective ingredients such as beans, rice, oats, frozen or canned vegetables, fruits, yogurt, and more that won't break your budget.

Finance and Health Connection

A 2015 survey found that most people viewed their financial and physical health as strongly linked. 81% of those who responded felt that their other goals became much easier to achieve when their finances were in good shape. Along the same lines, 70% said that good financial health positively impacted their physical health (The Connection Between Financial Health and Physical Well-Being). Healthy habits that we incorporate into our lives can affect our finances directly or indirectly. Career success doesn't mean much if you aren't taking care of your body to enjoy it. Even if better health isn't enough of an incentive, the financial benefits of prioritizing your health should be enough to persuade you to do so.

Chapter Summary

In this chapter, we discussed how poor health can affect you financially. Poor health can affect your insurance costs, medical expenses, and your ability to retire and live independently. The best course of action to tackle these situations is prevention and early lifestyle adoptions for healthier living. Also, prioritizing your health can affect you financially, including employer incentives, missing less time from work, and developing finance and health habits.

Chapter 6: Mastering Your Retirement Knowledge

Retirement wasn't something Amara was ready to think about in high school. She was only 18, and retirement was years down the road. Besides, thinking about "old people stuff" wasn't very cool.

Despite all of this, her parents continued to talk to her about teaching. She was a fantastic tutor at her school, and she loved to work with the kids at her local library and STEM clubs.

"And," they said one night, "you even get a teacher's retirement."

Amara didn't think anything of the retirement plan but decided to pursue her teaching career anyways.

Throughout college, she worked multiple jobs to keep up with her payments. Later in her senior year while she completed her student teaching, she worked night shifts and completed her homework on her breaks and between jobs.

The work was enough to make her want to give it up, but when she finally got her diploma, she was relieved to graduate and get a teaching job of her own. After months of preparation and work, she landed a job teaching at a nearby elementary school as soon as she got out of college.

Because of this, after only working for 35 years, Amara was able to retire with full benefits because of her decision to work for the school system. She was 57 when she said goodbye to work, and she felt that same relief she'd felt before walking across the graduation stage.

Now she had the time, the energy, and the money to spend time with her grandchildren and teach them as they grew up. It was thanks to her retirement plan that she was able to spend her years with her family rather than working.

Will you have enough money saved to live on for at least 20 to 30 years during retirement? While this question can cause some angst, those prepared for this moment in time won't have an issue. Planning for a comfortable retirement doesn't have to be complicated or an impossible task. Of course, it's much wiser to start sooner than later, but whenever you begin, you want to have an intelligent plan in place to reach your retirement goals.

Paying Yourself First (Retirement)

A fundamental of your retirement account is paying yourself first. The idea behind paying yourself first is straightforward and the same as saving for an emergency fund and your investment accounts. When you prioritize paying yourself first, you tell yourself your financial future is more important than any bill, debt, or random purchase you currently make. While retirement may not be here today eventually, it comes on the horizon for everyone. Therefore, making sure you are appropriately prepared for it should be one of your top financial priorities throughout your lifetime.

When To Start A Retirement Account

The short answer: as soon as you start working. Ideally, you would want to start in your twenties, though sometimes that may not be possible with how life plays out. Regardless, the younger you can begin, the better. Here are two reasons to consider to get you saving now:

1. Compound interest

Each year's gains can generate their own gains the next year—a powerful wealth-building phenomenon known as compounding. Thus, time in the market, along with consistent contributions, dictates the returns you could expect from your accounts.

2. Saving is a habit

It may seem logical to begin saving as early as possible, but it isn't always easy. However, the instinct to save grows as you do it. As you watch your account balance grow, it will begin to feel fantastic.

Savings By Age

So how much should you have saved? This is a unique question to each person and their lifestyle. Your lifestyle should reflect your savings goals and play a significant role in how you save now for retirement. To reach your goal, you can implement savings goals with specific target amounts and dates.

Goals by 30: Look to have 1x your income saved.

Goals by 40: Look to have 3x your income saved.

Goals by 50: Look to have 5x your income saved.

Goals by 60: Look to have 7x your income saved.

Goals by 70: Look to have 9x your income saved.

Please remember you should view this as more of a guide than a strict plan. The amount you should save for retirement should be based on factors including:

- Your income
- Your planned retirement age
- The kind of lifestyle you want to live in retirement

Looking at your savings in 10-year increments makes it easier to plan financially and put actionable savings steps in place. For example, aim to save between 5% to 15% of your income for retirement—or start with a manageable percentage for your budget and increase the amount 1% each year until you reach 15%.

Starting Late?

One strategy to reach your retirement savings goal is to make the most of your early years of employment. If you have less time to save for retirement, you will just have to save more each year. For example, if you have a goal of reaching $1 million at the age of 65 and saving about $4500 a year starting at 20, you have a good chance of meeting this goal. Start at 30, and you will have to save about $9000 a year. At 40 will take about $18000 a year. As we can see, starting later with retirement savings can be accomplished to reach a reasonable goal, but it will take a large portion of your livable income yearly to do so. So unless necessary, the best course of action is to start your retirement saving journey while young.

Debt Free Retirement

Hopefully, going into retirement debt-free is one aspect of your retirement goals that you have defined and prioritized as something to accomplish. Not having to worry about any debts or unfulfilled obligations, especially during retirement, can bring a tremendous feeling of relief to you in your golden years. However, life after debt can be extraordinary, and here are some reasons why it would be wise to alleviate any debt before you retire to achieve that life:

1. Reduces your nervousness

Major bills during retirement can cause a lot of anxiety and 'what if' thinking about money. What if I run out of money? What if I can't pay my mortgage? Having debt in retirement amplifies these financial worries. The most straightforward method to reducing this fear and nervousness is to take care of your debt before retiring. You won't regret it and probably will bring some peace, at least financially, to your life.

2. Learn to live within your means

Having debt has for a while now been pushed upon us as expected and a common way for us to purchase goods and just live normally. Debt is simply purchasing an item without having the money to do so and needing to borrow the money from a bank.

If you can't afford something and have to borrow to get it, you're living beyond your means. Again, this isn't a big concern when working, and you can afford the monthly payments. It does, however, become a strain in retirement. Stop borrowing money today (and pay off all you've already borrowed), and your retirement will be less stressful and more productive.

3. Eliminates interest payments

Living within your means can be the best way to eliminate any interests payments you are paying. Imagine the money saved on a 30-year mortgage or any personal loans or credit card debt. Instead of making others rich with your interest payments, consider paying down your debt and investing the money instead—giving yourself a better retirement outlook.

4. Improves cash flow

Another area where living within your means can improve your financial situation. Consider all the areas of debt you are making monthly payments; credit cards, your house, your car, personal loans, etc. Having all these areas paid off going into retirement can mean quite a bit of extra income at your disposal.

5. Reduces financial hassles

When you are in debt, there always seems to be some hassle or nuisance you have to consider. Either make sure you are not late on a monthly payment, having multiple debtors to consider repaying, or worrying about maintaining or improving your credit score by keeping up payments can be a drag. The best way to remove these hassles from your life is not to owe anyone any money. Life can become relatively simple when you take as many people as you may owe money out of it.

6. Easier to become wealthy

Distractions can be a significant obstacle to the discipline needed for building wealth. Juggling house debt, car loans, student loans, and various other payments can be constant distractions that can be removed by taking care of debt. It's just easier to build a nest egg going into retirement when your focus can be on stacking your money.

7. Allows clear decision making

A life with no debt becomes one where you can make decisions more clearly. For example, decisions on emergencies that may come up or splurging on a vacation can be made within reason and without having to put your life on hold because debts have your attention. It's ridiculous how many people get trapped in bad decisions because of debt and not taking care of it, especially going into retirement.

Chapter Summary

In this chapter, we discussed the importance of paying yourself first for your retirement accounts. These are the accounts you don't want to neglect in investing, as your livelihood in retirement depends on how you save now. In addition, we discussed how the sooner you start your retirement accounts, the sooner compound interest can work in your favor, and you can develop consistent saving habits. Finally, we also addressed how savings by your age will affect your overall retirement strategy.

Chapter 7: Mastering Financial Independence

Paul stepped back and looked at his accomplishments. A nice house, completely paid off. A brand new car straight from the lot. Sounds of his wife and kids playing in the pool in the backyard echoed to the front of the house.

It wasn't easy work. In fact, he could still smell the grease of the french fries and hear the sizzling of burgers from his first job at 16. Even before then, the beating sun from his summer job mowing lawns was essential to getting this house. Even after working for a fast food restaurant throughout high school, he still looked for more.

In between shifts, he tutored some friends on the basketball team for a few dollars a session. Later on in college, he expanded his tutoring sessions to those in his major field. He no longer worked at the fast food restaurant but instead worked for the school's mail room.

After college, he got a job at a nearby bank, working the front desk. During his lunch break, he began looking for investments to put his money into and researched trends. He moved up in the ranks at the bank, invested more, received more, and built his way up to financial independence.

Even after big life moments—like the wedding and the birth of his two children—he still had plenty of money set aside to turn a profit. In fact, he even used some of that money to help his children start investing in their own work, like buying them a new lawn mower and getting them a car at 16 so that they could drive to the libraries to tutor their friends.

He was even able to donate money to his local charities and groups to help better the community and set an example for his kids. Not only did they learn how to become financially independent later in life, they also learned how to use their money to invest in the community around them.

Paul smiled and sighed. Thanks to his knowledge and understanding of money, he was able to give his family a comfortable life and himself a bright future. Taking one last look at the work he was finally able to achieve, he went to join his family.

Perhaps the most crucial aspect of going through your financial independence journey is managing the wealth you've established and passing it on to future generations. Proper planning can establish financial prosperity that can benefit your family for generations if properly managed. That's why passing financial literacy knowledge to your kids is just as important as the money itself.

Building Generational Wealth

The concept of generational wealth isn't new. It's also known as "old money" or "family wealth." You probably have heard of popular family names like the Kennedys, Waltons, or the Rockefellers as examples of generational wealth. But you don't have to become mega-rich to create wealth that will last. Building generational wealth can be attainable with the will and correct knowledge to do so. Here are four practical methods to help you do so.

Create multiple sources of income

Start with full-time work

Full-time employment provides you with a steady source of income that can be funneled into savings and investing. Furthermore, it generally provides benefits like a 401k or Health Savings Account, which are great investment tools. However, your full-time job is not enough to create long-term wealth but is the starting point.

Get a side hustle

Side hustles have gained a lot of traction over the past few years, and for a good reason. They can significantly impact your income in the long run if you leverage your money and time wisely. The key to making the most of your cash flow from your side hustle is not to think of this as extra money. Instead, if you create the correct plan for this money, you can set up yourself and your family for a rewarding financial future.

Create passive income

In the traditional sense, passive income is money you don't have to work for. Investing can be the best generator of passive income, and the type of income generally wealthy individuals depend on.

Continue to learn new things

When learning how to invest, the more you put into it, the better you will become. Creating generational wealth is not a task for the idle. Therefore, it's essential to continue learning in investing and in general. Getting comfortable in a situation is the best way to lead to complacency. That complacency causes you to stop paying attention to how decisions affect your well-being and your family's well-being. So stay diligent in your learning, as keeping yourself up to date will impact your success as an investor and your happiness in other areas of your life.

Spend your money wisely

So we've established how to earn money consistently. Now we should establish how to hold on to it because no amount of money will keep someone foolish rich. Some typical money spending traps usually include:

- Not having enough in your emergency fund
- Not having enough money invested in the stock market
- Buying things you don't need

Avoiding these traps usually include:

- Paying yourself first

- Investing frequently in your investment and retirement accounts
- Thinking long term, doing your best to avoid short term material purchases

Start the journey to financial freedom now

It's time to start investing the money you've saved once you've gotten your spending under control. You have the know-how and can start right now. The quickest and easiest method to generate money over time is to start investing today. If you invest in companies with high compounding yearly rates of return, your money increases for you without you having to do anything! Expanding your knowledge for the progression of your financial freedom journey should also be a point of emphasis.

Keeping Generational Wealth

Keeping the wealth built over time takes strategy and the correct mindset. Those who have remained wealthy for generations, expanding their fortune and passing on even more to their offspring than they received, understand the importance of money.

Invest in your children's education

One of the best investments you can make is your child's education. Provide them with the education and resources they need to provide for themselves and their children.

While college may not be a path for all children, teaching them excellent work ethic and understanding they need to manage inherited wealth will still pay dividends. At the very least, this knowledge would be a solid base for building their own wealth.

Teach your kids about personal finance

Ask yourself, "What skills did you use to make money?" Hard work? Perseverance? Resourcefulness? Discipline? Teaching your children these habits either by example or by conversation trains them in the way to be responsible for handling any passed down wealth to them. Explanations and seeing things in person can be some of the best tools to provide them to be able to sustain and grow passed down wealth or wealth they generate.

Spend quality time with your children

Spending quality time with your children is not typically thought of as a way to keep generational wealth. Though watching their parents live the teachings they are teaching their children might be more beneficial than it is given credit for. Take the opportunity to teach them how money works and the value of saving and investing. Show them what kind of life financial planning can provide, and take the time to discuss how you got here.

Passing On Generational Wealth

An estate plan and will give you control over the wealth and well-being of your family after you pass away. By doing so you can ensure that your kids, grandkids, and future generations have the tools they need to take care of the wealth you made.

Create an estate plan and will

As you have worked hard to build wealth, you should have a lawyer help you design an estate plan to ensure that your wishes are carried out when you pass away. This will let your children and relatives know what needs to be done with the wealth. The will should encompass all your assets including investments, businesses, property, and any other valuables. The more specific you are with any distributions the less your kids or relatives have to worry about.

Setup custodial accounts

It's not necessary to leave your wealth to your children after you pass away. You can and should also set up custodial accounts on their behalf. A custodial account is an investment account that you manage until they reach adult age, typically age 18 or 21, and can be a great way to set money aside for your kid's future.

This money can be used for just about any financial goal you want to help your kids meet.

Name beneficiaries

Whenever you open a financial account, you have the option to name a beneficiary. The beneficiary is the person who will receive your funds upon your death. Naming a beneficiary is important and can relieve your family of unnecessary stress.

What steps are you taking to set up your family for a better financial future? Following this path and providing your heirs with everything they need to succeed in addition to the money itself will ensure a far more successful legacy for you and your family.

Chapter Summary

This chapter has explained generational wealth and how it's the culmination of your financial literacy journey. Building generational wealth consists of various aspects, including creating multiple income streams, continuing to learn new things, spending money wisely, and beginning the financial freedom journey as soon as possible. Keeping that wealth involves investing in your children's education, teaching your kids about personal finance, and spending quality time with your kids to enforce the knowledge you are passing down to them.

Final Words

Mastering your budget is the beginning of the journey. Getting your finances under control and developing the discipline to keep them under control takes time but once kept consistently brings stability to your purpose.

Mastering your emergency fund doesn't allow you to get sidetracked when life happens. Being prepared for the unexpected and not allowing lifestyle creep when you earn more money throughout your career doesn't derail the financial discipline you've been building.

Mastering your debt will enable you to keep more of the money you work so hard to make. In addition, knowing about the various types of debt and the advantages and disadvantages they bring to your financial situation enables you to address whether you won't take on any debt obligation or how to quickly and efficiently pay any off.

Mastering your investment knowledge gives you the blueprint on how to build your wealth. In addition, understanding the importance of paying yourself first and developing the discipline to practice paying yourself first consistently will be beneficial throughout your lifetime.

Mastering your health can be the best investment you can make in your lifetime. This is because that knowledge of how health affects finances and vice versa is so valuable. When you prioritize your health, you prioritize your wealth.

Mastering your retirement sets up your life for when your working career is over. So paying yourself first here will benefit you as you are living on the money you focused on for retirement—ideally, compounding working in our favor because of our discipline putting money in our accounts.

Mastering financial independence; is it even possible? Of course, and you can achieve it by adopting and mastering the topics this book has covered!

Thank You

There is a lot that goes into completing a book. The team that I've worked with and the people involved with the message of this guide have really helped bring this book to life. I'd like to thank all those who worked on the manuscript and took the time to understand the vision.

Thank you to the editors and those who advised me on how to convey the content of the book. I'd also like to thank my mentors, family, and friends for guiding and inspiring me while I worked on this latest guide. Your unwavering support helped the process and made the publication of *Mastering Financial Independence* possible.

I would also like to thank my supporters who bought my previous book *Achieving Your Financial Breakthrough*. If you liked the information from this book, then you will want to read this one as well. It goes into more detail about your future plans and how to improve your quality of life by breaking through financial barriers.

To all who read this book, and to those who will read others to come, I thank you.

References

Buchenau, Z. (n.d.), *Why is budgeting important? 10 Key benefits.* Be the Budget. https://bethebudget.com/why-is-budgeting-important/

The connection between financial health & physical well-being. (n.d.). Invest Blue. https://www.investblue.com.au/knowledge-centre/fact-sheets/the-connection-between-financial-health-physical-well-being

Consumer Financial Protection Bureau. (2017 January 30). *Are there laws that limit what debt collectors can say or do?* Consumer Finance. https://www.consumerfinance.gov/ask-cfpb/are-there-laws-that-limit-what-debt-collectors-can-say-or-do-en-329/

Danielsson, M. (2022 January 11). *These 12 habits will help you reach financial freedom.* Investopedia. https://www.investopedia.com/articles/personal-finance/112015/these-10-habits-will-help-you-reach-financial-freedom.asp

Ellen, R. (2019 September 11). *What is the ideal age of money?* You Need a Budget. https://www.youneedabudget.com/what-is-the-ideal-age-of-money/

Epperson, S., Dickler, J. (2020 January 27). *The secret to financial success: Paying off debt.* CNBC. https://www.cnbc.com/2020/01/27/how-to-pay-off-debt.html

Folger, J. (2021 February 21). *Five rules to improve your financial health.* Investopedia. https://www.investopedia.com/articles/personal-finance/111813/five-rules-improve-your-financial-health.asp

Fogler, J. (2022 January 26). *How to manage lifestyle inflation.* Investopedia. https://www.investopedia.com/articles/personal-finance/092313/how-manage-lifestyle-inflation.asp

Foster, S. (2021 July 21). *Survey: More than half of Americans couldn't cover three months of expenses with an emergency fund.* Bankrate. https://www.bankrate.com/banking/savings/emergency-savings-survey-july-2021/

Four simple rules for successful budgeting. (n.d.). You Need a Budget. https://www.youneedabudget.com/the-four-rules/

Harkness, B. (2021 January 8). *How to pay off debt: 6 strategies that work.* Credit Card Insider. https://www.creditcardinsider.com/learn/reducing-debt/

The importance of having an emergency fund. (n.d.). TIAA. https://www.tiaa.org/public/offer/insights/managing-your-money/the-importance-of-having-an-emergency-fund

The Investopedia Team. (2021 March 8). *What are the main categories of debt?* Investopedia. https://www.investopedia.com/ask/answers/110614/what-are-main-categories-debt.asp

Johnston, J. (2021 December 1). *How to set and achieve financial goals.* Incharge. https://www.incharge.org/financial-literacy/budgeting-saving/how-to-set-financial-goals/

Kagan, J. (2021 October 29). *Consumer debt.* Investopedia. https://www.investopedia.com/terms/c/consumer-debt.asp

Kenton, W. (2021 December 30). *Fair Debt Collection Practices Act (FDCPA).* Investopedia. https://www.investopedia.com/terms/f/fair-debt-collection-practices-act-fdcpa.asp

LaPonsie, M. (2021 March 29). *Should young adults really be saving for retirement?* U.S. News. https://money.usnews.com/money/retirement/401ks/articles/should-young-adults-really-be-saving-for-retirement

Linton, A. (2021 June 27). *Saving goals and retirement milestones.* The Balance. https://www.thebalance.com/money-milestones-you-need-to-hit-at-every-age-4147835

Levitt, A. (2021 September 29). *Why should I pay myself first?* Investopedia. https://www.investopedia.com/ask/answers/12/pay-yourself.asp

Melissa. (2014 February 10). *Take care of your health now to grow and preserve your wealth.* Bible Money Matters. https://www.biblemoneymatters.com/take-care-of-your-health-now-to-grow-and-preserve-your-wealth/

Mercadante, K. (2021 August 11). *How to invest in your 20s: 8 Invest ideas for young adults.* Investor Junkie. https://investorjunkie.com/investing/investments-to-consider-while-young/#8-improve-your-skills

Net worth calculator. (n.d.). Bankrate. https://www.bankrate.com/calculators/smart-spending/personal-net-worth-calculator.aspx

Page, J. F. (n.d.). *The 70% rule: Afford spending, saving, and investing on any income!* Fun Cheap or Free. https://funcheaporfree.com/the-70-percent-rule/

Pant, P. (2021 December 9). *The difference between wants and needs.* The Balance. https://www.thebalance.com/how-to-separate-wants-and-needs-453592

Park, T. (2021 December 25). *Best retirement strategies for your 20s.* The Balance. https://www.thebalance.com/best-retirement-strategies-for-your-20s-4177587

Pyles, S. (2020 May 29). *How to pay off debt fast: 7 Tips.* Nerd Wallet. https://www.nerdwallet.com/article/finance/find-extra-money-pay-debts

Ramsey Solutions. (2021 November 5). *What is debt consolidation?* Ramsey Solutions. https://www.ramseysolutions.com/debt/debt-consolidation-truth#authorbio

Rose, J. (2022 January 4). *The top 10 good financial goals that everyone should have for 2022.* Good Financial Cents. https://www.goodfinancialcents.com/good-financial-goals/

Sall, D. (2018 May 17). *Debt free retirement! 7 Reasons to pay off every penny before you retire.* New Retirement. https://www.newretirement.com/retirement/debt-free-retirement-7-reasons-pay-off-every-penny-before-you-retire/

Sanchez, L. (2018 May 8). *The importance of investing when you're young.* Millennial Wealth. https://millennialwealthllc.com/importance-of-investing-when-youre-young/

Sarah. (2022 February 7). *How to avoid lifestyle inflation: 9 Key ways.* Clever Girl Finance. https://www.clevergirlfinance.com/blog/lifestyle-inflation/

Savings by age: How much to save in your 20s, 30s, 40s, and beyond. (2021 June 24). Ally. https://www.ally.com/do-it-right/money/savings-by-age-how-much-to-save-in-your-20s-30s-40s-and-beyond/

Town, P. (n.d.). *How to build generational wealth and keep it!* Rule One Investing. https://www.ruleoneinvesting.com/blog/financial-control/generational-wealth/

Underwood, K. (2022 January 17). *Financial reasons to prioritize your health.* Due. https://due.com/blog/financial-reasons-to-prioritize-your-health/

Vohwinkle, J. (2022 January 14). *What is net worth?* The Balance. https://www.thebalance.com/what-is-your-net-worth-1289788

Wade, J. (2021 May 17). *The best way to start investing when you're young.* Investing Answers. https://investinganswers.com/articles/ask-expert-whats-best-way-start-investing-when-youre-young

What are the different types of debt? (n.d.). Equifax. https://www.equifax.com/personal/education/debt-management/types-of-consumer-debts/

What's the right emergency fund amount? (n.d.). Vanguard. https://investor.vanguard.com/investor-resources-education/emergency-fund/whats-the-right-emergency-fund-amount

When should I start saving for retirement? (n.d.). CNN Money. https://money.cnn.com/retirement/guide/basics_basics.moneymag/index.htm

When should you start saving for retirement? (n.d.). Vanguard. https://investor.vanguard.com/retirement/savings/when-to-start

Whiteside, E. (2020 October 28). *WHat is the 50/20/30 budget rule?* Investopedia. https://www.investopedia.com/ask/answers/022916/what-502030-budget-rule.asp